The Country Life Picture Book of

IRELAND

Elgy Gillespie

Country Life Books

frontispiece
Clifden (see page 76)

Published by Country Life Books
and distributed for them by
The Hamlyn Publishing Group Limited
London·New York·Sydney·Toronto
Astronaut House, Feltham, Middlesex, England

First published 1980

ISBN 0 600 34921 7

Set in 12 on 14 pt Monophoto Ehrhardt by
Tradespools Limited, Frome
Colour separations made by
Culver Graphics Litho Limited, High Wycombe
Printed in Italy

Introduction

It is an odd thing, but Ireland has always had an influence on the world which is much greater than her physical size would suggest. You might laugh and reply that the Romans never bothered to conquer her and that, so far as Europe was concerned, she was out on the very edge of the world's end, trembling on the brink of unknown horrors until Columbus made his voyage – and proved that there was a New World beyond.

None of that would be quite true, and it is not only the Irish who claim a greater significance for their small and waterlogged home. Four of the signatories of the American Declaration of Independence were of Irish birth, another nine of Irish ancestry. The founders of the American, the Peruvian and the Argentinian navies were Irish. The liberator and first president of Chile was Irish. All other Latin-American countries, as well as Canada and Australasia, can number Irish among their famous men. Today there are more Irish in England than there are in Dublin and four times as many in the United States as in the whole island. Ireland supplied most of the Restoration playwrights who made the eighteenth-century Londoners laugh, as well as writers from Swift and Goldsmith to Wilde, Yeats, O'Casey, Joyce and Beckett – and she also exports footballers and comedians.

Ireland's literal isolation forced even her earliest people to travel and to forge continental links. The periods of her greatest wealth and influence were when she was at her most xenophiliac, when most inclined to trade ideas and goods with other countries. The first golden epoque was her Early Bronze Age, from the eighteenth to the fifteenth century BC, when she was one of Europe's best-known suppliers of gold and bronze-crafted arms and ornaments. The finest of these can still be seen in Dublin at the National Museum.

The next golden age was during the fifth, sixth and seventh centuries, when Ireland's early Christian monks managed to hang on to some of the Roman learning that was perishing as the barbarians overran Europe. They developed and preserved this in the cultural centres of their monasteries, and their missionary monks took it back to Charlemagne and his Frankish kingdoms. The Book of Durrow, an illuminated gospel of the seventh century ($c.650$), and the Book of Kells ($c.800$), over a century younger but most gorgeous of all, are relics of the timeless peace enjoyed by these distant monks. You may see both in the Old Library of Trinity College, where their pages are turned once a day – so that if you visited the Book of Kells daily you would eventually be able to read it all.

The last age that could be described as truly golden, if only for some – and there is still a lot of argument about this – was the last part of the eighteenth century, from the time of Henry Grattan's parliament until the Act of Union which fused the island to London began to take effect. The finest architecture still left standing dates from this liberal and expansive age, when Catholics were enjoying a considerable measure of freedom and trades flourished.

Of course there were reasons other than trade for travel: reasons like famine, religious or political intolerance, lack of land or lack of work. The 'Flight of the Earls' in 1607, when the great chieftains O'Neill and O'Donnell forfeited all their lands to King James's men and fled to the Continent, is one reason why you will find many Irish names in Galicia and other parts of Spain. Later on, after the Treaty of Limerick, the defeated opponents of King William emigrated to France and Spain; they were known as the 'Wild Geese'.

But it was the Great Famine of the last century which most dramatically altered the country's prospects. Boat after boat took off for America filled with starving homeless people – and sometimes they were sent back again from their destination, and, in one instance at least, anchored off Liverpool while cholera raged along the decks. This goes some way

A page from the Book of Kells.

towards explaining the peculiarly virile nationalism of the American Irish, often so difficult for the Irish Irish and the English Irish to understand.

Altogether the Famine succeeded in shrinking the population from at least $8\frac{1}{2}$ million in 1840 to a mere $4\frac{1}{2}$ million now – and this is a steady improvement on the fifties, when emigration in this century reached a new peak. Sad to say, neither independence nor Mr de Valera's policies nor Ireland's neutrality in the last war brought any blush of prosperity for the mass of the people. The fifties saw an Ireland that was still small, still waterlogged and still essentially agricultural, exporting her young people like her cattle – on the hoof.

Traditionally it was the most able children who took the emigrant's farewell – or took to the priesthood instead, sometimes in return for an education. But of course it was also the workless and those in trouble who left. This, too, affected the population, but these days it is on the up and up again, by 1·2 per cent a year. Since the expanding sixties, for the first time in history there have been more Irish people living in cities than on the land. Though unemployment is still chronic and wavers around the 9 per cent mark (the highest rate in the EEC, bar only Northern Ireland's 12–13 per cent), her young people now emigrate because they want to, and not simply to avoid starvation.

You might say that Ireland has changed far more economically and socially in the past fifteen years than in the previous fifteen hundred, and they are changes which have often caught her out. Up until now an average Irishman's idea of what it means to be Irish was quite simple if he happened to be a Southerner: a practising Catholic of unswerving patriotism and a loyalty to the Gaelic games like hurling, handball and Gaelic football, and to the Gaelic language, even if he had forgotten most of the Irish that was stuffed into him at school.

For the remaining 3 per cent of Protestants in the South and the Protestant majority in the North of Ireland, this wasn't a very handy recipe of course. Nowadays Ireland is teetering on a watershed, Europeanised so far as prices and expectations go, but with her roads and her communications still poor, her industries still just beginning, her resources still untapped or tapped by others. She is almost unique in that you still cannot divorce here, petition for an abortion on any grounds or buy contraceptives at present. A process of painful and difficult self-examination and cross-questioning is going on, evidenced by the conflicting ideas being tossed about. A new definition of what it means to be Irish must eventually emerge, and like all births it will probably hurt.

'Irish' is a word with lots of connotations across the water, some of them comic and some of them not so comic. There are all the Irish jokes, which Irishmen make about Kerrymen – and probably for the same reasons. (Sample: 'What does a Kerryman call his pet zebra?' Answer: 'Spot.') The Irish have to grin and bear them, realising that their function is to siphon off aggression. But they do carry along further the connotations.

In the earliest, barely English, medieval poetry it is interesting to find that those connotations were alive and well even then. A fourteenth-century pop song scrawled on the margin of a manuscript already indicates an image of a broth of a boy, somehow combined with slightly self-conscious piety:

> *Icham of Irlaunde,*
> *Ant of the holy londe*
> *Of Irlande.*
> *Gode sire, pray ich ye,*
> *For of saynte charité,*
> *Come ant daunce wyt me*
> *In Irlaunde.*

Perhaps the Irishman was already translating himself in a special export edition for foreigners,

because when that was written the Gaelic poets had long established a tradition of nature poetry and divine poetry in their own language, including the oldest and most mysterious poem of all, the one that starts:

I am the wind which breathes upon the sea,
I am the wave of the ocean,
I am the murmur of the billows . . .

The poet who wrote that (and it may have been written before Christ's birth; the date is uncertain) may have been the earliest poet in any land on this continent other than Greece. The scholar and Irish president Douglas Hyde thought so. Later on these languages were coexisting but scarcely mingling: Anglo-Norman, Anglo-Saxon and Gaelic. Gaelic was the oldest by a very, very long way, and it is still alive among the 55,000 who speak it today, though largely confined as a genuine everyday language to the Gaeltacht pockets along the west coast. It is easy to forget that English as a vernacular tongue is barely three centuries old in Ireland and that Irish was spoken throughout the country, though heavily frowned upon, until the end of the last century. It lives on today among lovers of the language and as the bane and curse of the average schoolchild's life, though it has been much abused in politics.

But the Irish language is just one facet of a culture that is profoundly different and often difficult for foreigners to understand. Of course, the culture is virtually always conveyed in English now and for the average Irishman to hear Irish colloquially spoken would be a little bit as though an Englishman were to go to Cirencester and hear pure Anglo-Saxon spoken – in terms of excitement and culture shock, if not of probability – were it not for the fact that the language has developed through the centuries and is now modern Irish.

Culture is built from history, recorded and unrecorded, and the social conditions and economy of a place. But behind that are all sorts of other things – the weather, the crops, the seas. And behind that again is the geography, the landscape of it all. If we look at these now, we will get lots of clues to the culture and the people.

*　　*　　*

With her ragged west coast, and her tamer east coast still at two removes from the Continent, Ireland rounds off the Atlantic fringes of north-western Europe. She is the smaller one of two major offshore islands acting as outposts to the mainland. Some people compare her shape to a puppy standing on his hind paws to beg for attention. Her crumpled edges – sometimes mountainous and rocky – roughly encircle a limestone lowland of raised bog and water-filled hollows, a mere 32,595 square miles altogether.

At no point can the traveller in Ireland be more than seventy miles from the sea, and it is possible to drive from any place to another within the span of a day. She is a mere eleven miles from Scotland at her closest point, and at one stage in the last century Dissenting Northerners used to row across to Kintyre for the kirk each Sunday. Ireland only detached herself at the end of the last Ice Age, when rising sea water cut the cord less than 10,000 years ago.

It was across the narrow bridge of land from Kintyre that the flora and the fauna came – and some of them never quite made it. There are no moles, voles, toads, snakes or any reptiles other than the common lizard. It was St Patrick who banished the snakes from Ireland according to the alternative version – and though a schoolboy of my acquaintance used to buy two grass snakes from a pet shop and send them off together into the sunset, snakes have never been found wild here since.

St Patrick, by the way, was a Romanised British Celt who was brought to Ireland as a boy slave. He was not the first Christian to set foot on Irish soil:

Palladius from Rome is supposed to have been the first according to a manuscript which dates his arrival as 431. But by that time it is highly likely that returning traders had brought Christianity back from Wales and England. Though the Romans did not invade Ireland, there must have been plenty of to-ing and fro-ing between the two islands, or Hibernia and Britannia as the Romans called them.

But to return to the end of the Ice Age: the melting waters did more than just cut the island adrift from her umbilical cord. They are generally held responsible for the familiarly wet climate which gave birth to the bogs of peat – or turf, as they call it in the North – and altogether these cover one sixth of the island's surface. Sometimes the peat bogs are found stretching for miles at a time across the low-lying limestone midlands. At other times you will find them among the thin-soiled and impoverished uplands of Connemara, Mayo, Sligo and Donegal. In summer they will be yellow with gorse and purple with heather and loud with the song of well-fed bees.

It is true that in Ireland you can tell summer has come when the rain gets warmer. Even in the sunniest months – May and June – a mere $5\frac{1}{2}$ to $6\frac{1}{2}$ hours of sunshine a day are enjoyed at the outside. You can load the odds up to an average 7 hours a day if you go to the sunny south-east, where strawberries and the tillage of wheat and beet and the fattest cattle thrive. Here you will find a special sort of honey: the clover honey for which County Wexford and the valleys of the Slaney and the Barrow are renowned. But it has to be faced that the famous forty shades of green would not exist did not the annual rainfall consistently exceed its recorded minimum of thirty inches a year, and we would not have our fat beef, our rich milk and butter (and recently cheese and yoghurt) and our long pastoral tradition, our intimacy with land so often stirred by quarrels over it from the very beginning.

It is also true that the Gulf Stream which touches the south-western tips of counties Kerry and Cork brings them arbutus and magnolias, not to mention the palms that line the water's edge at Glengariff, and the ubiquitous fuchsia. It also brings a very rich variety of bryophytes and lichens. These counties are among the wettest parts of the country. As in the rocky outcrops of Connemara, and the yet more mist-enshrouded and untrammelled wild peaks of Donegal, and the bare grey rocks of the Burren, with its rare wild flowers like the alpine gentian and the dense-flowered orchid (now disappearing in the face of new insecticides), and the sodden Ring of Kerry where in 1903 they once measured 141 inches of rain in a year, and the friendly little hills of Wicklow: Wet is Beautiful.

Weather can be blamed for an awful lot in Ireland. Certain climatologists concluded that it was the weather most conducive to hard work, in which case it was silly of them not to pass the message on to the occupants. While it is true that you will never find a country nearer to the weather and you will never find a subject more fascinating or exasperating in a climate so changeable, the distinguished geologist who writes that 'the constantly changing weather brings a sense of uncertainty and perhaps encourages an indifference to time and a predilection towards gambling and alcohol' may be overdoing it a little.

In Donegal they say the weather is their protection against being overrun by tourists. They are undoubtedly right. In record-breaking summers like that of 1976 the entire population is transformed into merry Greeks and the unspoiledness seems miraculous; but such summers are rare.

What certain geologists claim is that if it were not for Ireland and its Gulf Stream, Scotland would be permanently iced over and reduced to an Arctic landscape. But it is not for this reason alone that a certain archaeologist named Macalister used to say that England had cause to be thankful that Ireland existed. 'If Ireland were entirely submerged', he said, 'the people of England – subjected to the climate that now afflicts Ireland – would immediately begin to develop all those shortcomings which they are now so ready to find in the Irish!'

That is a theory to rank with a certain famous soldier's heartfelt wish that he could swop the populations of Holland and Ireland with each other, so that the Irish in Holland would drown and the Dutch in Ireland feed the world! Inevitably the smaller island has known a long and tormented relationship with the bigger one next door; inevitably the smaller one has defined herself in terms of when and how often the bigger one dominated her. But it is in the north-eastern part of Ireland – the nearest, and socially the oldest, if geologically the youngest – that you will find the closest and most symbiotic of relationships with 'across the water'. In ancient times there was even an Irish colony in Scotland – Dalriada, the nearest thing Ireland ever had to an empire.

Even the look of the north-east is such as would make any Scottish Highlander feel at home. The ancient Caledonian mountain ranges score the north-eastern (and the north-western) part of Ireland deeply, but in Derry and Antrim the dramatic folds have been covered with layers of black molten lava, now very weathered and split. Donegal relates directly to the Caledonian ranges, a relationship reinforced socially by her migrant potato-pickers who cross over each year.

All over, the island bares the largest stretch of carboniferous limestone in the whole of Europe; but the top layer – normally coal-bearing – has been stripped away by rain and wind to its present undulating grass meadows and bogs, leaving the Irish without the fuel that did so much to alter England's industrial history.

Yet, smothered in the black lava, the north-east held on to the chalky top layer, also full of flints and revealed in section along her famously scenic

'Where the mountains of Mourne sweep down
to the sea . . .'

coastline. This is a colder part of the country where things grow later and not so well. But the chalky top layer stuffed abundantly with flints beneath the black lava would have been visible to those early Mesolithic people who came to stay – and it may well have been the flints that lured them, for it was by these flints that these earliest peoples lived, striking the edges till they resembled leaf-shaped blades for cutting plants or flesh, even using them for fishing spears when tied on to sticks. The 'giant Irish elk', with his mighty antlers, may finally have been wiped out by these early hunters and gatherers. You may see a skeleton of this huge deer (wearing a plaster on his broken left leg) in the hallway of a lecture building in Trinity College, Dublin, and others in the Natural History Museum. You will find the best array of flints in the Ulster Museum, Belfast.

Perhaps if one could have given the hunters and gatherers a weather forecast they would not have bothered to come to Ireland: 'It will rain almost continuously till the end of time, with perhaps a slight letting-up in the early Bronze Age. In summer the temperatures will on occasion soar into the high sixties.' But they did come, and they are known as Larnians, after the County Antrim beach where their flints and emptied oyster shells are found in large numbers. The flints are also called 'Bann flakes', after the valley of the River Bann where an abundance of them can be seen in the cracking of the lava plateau that gave the waters of the largest inland lake, Lough Neagh, an exit to the sea.

There are people who claim that in these geological differences lie the root causes for the cultural gap between the north-east and the rest of the island. There are even those who say that the harsh temperatures and inhospitable landscape give Northerners their hard-working and industrious natures! Whatever of that, the sheer proximity has granted it closest links with Scotland, and these are reflected in the speech patterns, the farming

methods, the baking habits (potato cakes, soda farls and shortbread are familiar to those on both sides of the North Channel), and the Dissenters' religion, co-existing as in Scotland with the Catholic.

Some archaeologists have disputed that these Larnians were the first men, arriving in 6800 to 4000 BC, or thereabouts. Some support the claim that a skeleton found at Kilgreany in Waterford dates from as early as 9000 BC, during the Palaeolithic era, when men were painting wild boars on the walls of the caves at Lascaux in France. Never mind. What is certain is that the Ireland the Larnians knew was thickly forested with ash, oak, elm, alder, willow, mountain ash, hazel, holly and blackthorn – all of which were to survive till the sixteenth century, when landlords found it profitable to strip them. This is why Ireland is a bare and windswept isle on the whole, save for the ancient deciduous woods that are protected by the Forestry Commission.

Nowadays conifers or pines of all kinds from other latitudes are being planted in reafforestation schemes; they look oddly out of place. The hawthorn that annually drapes hedgerows across the land like a bridal veil is beginning to go too, as part of rigorous land-improvement. In olden days it was always thought unlucky to pick hawthorn; like thorn trees, it belonged to the fairies.

Sometimes the hedges are sprinkled with old clothes. This is a sure sign of a nearby settlement of tinkers. Nobody knows exactly when and how these very distinctive people, who are not gipsies but who are nomadic and have their own language, took to the 'long road'. Nowadays they have lost their old trades of pot-mending and horse-dealing and are reduced to begging.

The very first farmers followed on the Larnians before 3000 BC, and they were the first of the forest-clearers too. These men of the New Stone Age made themselves polished axes to split and work wood and cut down trees to plant crops. At

Ballynagilly in County Tyrone ten years ago, new excavations brought exciting evidence in the form of one of their square houses with two hearths, some pottery, two arrowheads – all radiocarbon-dated to around 3675 BC.

Similar but not quite such ancient houses were found at Lough Gur in County Limerick and again at Ballycastle in County Mayo, where Dr Michael Herity and Seamus Caulfield of University College, Dublin, recently uncovered the oldest plough ridges, showing a pretty advanced knowledge of agricultural techniques.

In the north we can see the burial places of these early farmers, in the shape of court cairns and also the portal tombs or dolmens, of which there are over a hundred examples – the best-known at Proleek in Louth or Kilclooney More near Ardara in Donegal. Dolmens have come to symbolise the ancient culture, with their massive uprights topped with a mighty capstone. It has been suggested that they often show alignments with the solstices on certain days of the year – so the farmers may have used them to work out when to plant crops, as well as for the burial of their dead.

Better known still are the cross-shaped passage graves with their strangely tooled and carved interiors. The biggest cluster of these megalithic passage tombs is in the Boyne Valley in County Meath; again they show signs of having a calendar significance for the farmer. At Newgrange, for instance, archaeologists have kept all-night vigils to prove that the first ray of sunlight will hit the furthest stone within only on the shortest day of the year (21 December), through a ceiling-slit over the entrance known as a 'roof-box'. Obviously the tomb-builders attached some religious or ritualistic significance to this – and perhaps to their spiral and zigzag carvings too – but what? Newgrange is near a vast stone circle, of the kind that were commonly built in the Bronze Age, and again, these afforded people a kind of calendar and astronomical

observatory by giving them alignments on certain days and nights of the year. Clearly these people were far more skilled than we once believed.

The miners and metalworkers who gave the Bronze Age its name thrived from about 1750 BC until the fifth century before Christ – and among them were a people named after Beaker ware, a kind of skilled pottery that archaeologists are finding more and more often, principally at Mount Gabriel in western Cork and in Wicklow. But the gold that the metalworkers used was panned from streams in the Wicklow hills, and their copper came from mines that you can inspect, perfectly preserved by bog over the centuries, near Mount Gabriel. Their jewellery – gold twisted earrings, spiral bracelets, dress fasteners – was exquisite, and their swords and halberds have been rescued, long-buried, from bogs and rivers. Their trade extended to North Africa.

You might say that the cultural movements of Europe were flinging out their waves, waves which were sometimes mere ripples by the time they neared Ireland and often did not quite make it to the shore. The Romans, the Saxons and Baroque architecture never actually arrived, though their influences percolated through. Megalithic tomb-builders, the Celts, the Vikings, the Normans, the Planters or colonists of Queen Elizabeth's time – all came to stay. As a rule these last got into Ireland through the fifty-mile gap in the coastal mountains around Dublin, which let them into the broad and rich plains of County Meath.

It was always easy for invaders to get a toehold, for Ireland was never united and organised against them, and they would always find allies among some of the warring tribes. And once the invaders came they stayed, because there was no further outpost to go to, and became subtly permeated with the Atlantic air: a process described as *'ipse hibernior hiberniis'*, 'becoming more Irish than the Irish'.

So the Celts eventually reached these shores, probably in small marauding bands of men, after

they had straddled the mainland of Europe. Perhaps
the people they found in Ireland were already
speaking an ancestor of the Gaelic language;
perhaps the Celts brought it with them. It is to the
Celts that Irishmen look back when they want to
remember an Ireland of kings and heroes and noble
deeds. The ancient myths and legends of Ireland are
embedded in this pre-Christian Iron Age, and it is
here we find the roots of great sagas like 'The Cattle
Raid of Cooley' and other heroic tales. So inevitably
our picture of the Celts and their glories is the
picture that the Celts themselves wanted to give us.

But many art historians feel the supreme
achievement of Celtic Ireland was the so-called La
Tène culture, which arrived here at least two
centuries later than in central Europe but here
flowered into a particularly sophisticated form of
metalwork and stone-ornamentation, of which the
stone of Turoe near Loughrea and the stone of
Mullaghmast in the National Museum are shining
examples.

This was also the era of the stone forts – like
Dún Aengus on the Aran Islands and the Grianán
of Ailech – and of the ringforts and the
crannog-dwellers: people who lived in pallisaded
lake houses on stilts. You can see a reconstructed
version at Craggaunowen in Clare of both a ringfort
and a crannog.

In a loose sort of a way the island was divided into
roughly 150 local kingdoms or *tuatha*, which were
ruled by overkings, who in their turn came under
the sway of five strong provincial kingdoms. There
was a legal system which dictated the rights and the
obligations of each person, and these rights
increased with a person's position in society, and
this in turn depended on his rank or position in the
fine or the extended family system. The poets, the
lawyers and the historians, etc., had known rights
and positions. There were pagan priest-kings as at
Tara and, if one is to believe the poets, the men of
Ulster are preserving their warrior-like

Cashel on its rock.

independence behind their barrier of hills against the men of Ireland even now!

This was the scene when Christianity gradually seeped in with Patrick and his predecessors. The bishops that Patrick created throughout the island were matched by the great number of monasteries that became bastions of recorded culture and schools for missionary monks – many of which you can still see, like the monastic city at Glendalough in Wicklow or a college like St Enda's at Killeany, on Inishmore Island. The little beehive cells for hermits and scholar monks scatter the loneliest places of the country, including many of the rumoured 365 islands in Clew Bay (High Island, Cahir Island and Owey Island among them) and the virtually uninhabitable crags in the sea like Skellig Michael off Kerry or Inishmurray off Sligo.

Life went on quite peaceably for centuries, unless you count the local feudings. While missionaries continued to spread the gospel abroad and manuscripts were laboriously written and illuminated, the O'Neills of the north controlled the secular world.

It must indeed have been a rude shock when in about 795 the Vikings arrived in their longboats, intent on sacking and raiding and extending their empire. Their booty included treasures from Irish monasteries, which occasionally still come to light in Viking graves back in Scandinavia today. In Dunmore Caves near Castlecomer in Kilkenny you may see some of the coins that the Viking raiders dropped from the little purses they kept in their armpits; they include an Arabic dirham, proof that their trading links extended as far as the Middle East.

In places like Wexford you can see exactly how the Vikings liked to arrange their towns, with lanes connecting their abattoirs to their jetties. One such lane still exists in Wexford and no less a person than the King of Norway commented on the linguistic origins of the name 'Keyser's Lane'. In Dublin, at Wood Quay, Viking houses, workshops, cesspits and storehouses have been excavated in front of Christ Church. Towns, as well as coinage and boatbuilding techniques, were the main innovations that the Vikings brought: Dublin, Wicklow, Arklow, Wexford, Waterford, Cork and Limerick were all founded by the marauders, and there is a sizeable amount of Viking blood in the racial make-up as well as in many Irish surnames.

The victory of Brian Boru against the massed forces of Vikings at Clontarf in 1014 was not a clean case of smashing the Viking sway since intermarriage already meant that it was difficult to say where 'Norse' influence ended and 'Irish' began. The excavators near Christ Church have had to coin a new word, 'Hiberno-Norse', while they try to work this one out. It is becoming more and more obvious during the course of these discoveries in Dublin that the Viking settlement was as important to them as York.

Dermot Mac Murrough is the man usually blamed for the Norman invasion, because it was the dethroned Dermot of Leinster who ran to Henry II in England, squealing for help to trounce his rivals and get the high kingship as well as his Leinster crown again. Henry had already been given permission to invade Ireland by the English pope of the time, Adrian IV, whose ears were full of the complaints of Irish sinfulness brought him by fulminating Irish missionaries. So Henry gave Dermot leave to recruit volunteer mercenaries, and Dermot did his recruiting among the ragamuffin, broken-down, fortune-hunting and illegitimate Normans hiding out in south Wales. In spite of their low status within the Norman world, these mercenaries were infinitely better organised in the military sense than the Irish; they wore conical helmets and armour and rode on horseback and, like Henry himself, spoke French – because they generally were French.

Dermot chose the Earl of Pembroke, otherwise

known as 'Strongbow', for his chief invader and promised him the hand of his daughter Aoife in marriage, as well as the kingship of Leinster. It is this scene rather than any other scene from history which is held up to schoolchildren as an example of Irish shame, as depicted in Daniel Maclise's famous picture of them all in Dublin's National Gallery. The wedding took place in Waterford, a city which is still full of very visible Norman and Viking relics – Reginald's Tower down by the sea, now converted into a civic museum, being the most famous.

Henry followed on the new invaders, and after quickly consecrating an abbey at Selskar in Wexford town, he pressed on up to Dublin, where he granted more lands to the Church in memory of the martyred Thomas à Becket, where Thomas Street is today. Then the sharing-out of the spoils began. But the sheer speed of the Norman conquest explained its shakiness in the next two centuries; at any rate, the new arrivals were rapidly absorbed into the Irish habits and lifestyle. By the fifteenth century only a small area, known as 'The Pale', around the proud and strictly organised medieval community in Dublin remained English.

This state of affairs came to an abrupt end when the Fitzgeralds' revolt failed and the Geraldine cause (as it was known) fell with the head of brave but foolhardy young 'Silken' Thomas Fitzgerald in 1536. After that Henry VIII adopted the title 'King of Ireland', and his subjects had cause to be resentful about the dissolution of the monasteries and the booty it yielded him. During the Middle Ages the big Cistercian, Dominican, Augustinian and Franciscan monasteries and friaries had enjoyed independence and prosperity, side by side with the proud Gaelicised families in their massive castles and tower houses. Now all that came to an end.

Queen Elizabeth hit upon a scheme for curtailing any quasi Home Rule. She invited the young sons of the greatest chieftains to live in her court and pick up English ways, in the hope that they would forget their Irish ones and become instruments of her power. But in the case of the young Hugh O'Neill this did not work; with O'Donnell he rose in revolt, for a time enjoying some success against Elizabeth's army, which was putting down risings with increasing brutality in order to make way for the Queen's settling 'Planters', one of whom, Sir Walter Raleigh, wound up with 40,000 ill-gotten acres and a house in the pretty seaside town of Youghal which is still there today. After the final defeat of O'Neill and the 'Flight of the Earls', when O'Neill, Rory O'Donnell and about a hundred of the nobility of Ulster fled to France from Rathmullen in Donegal, Catholics found their ways of life increasingly proscribed. By the late seventeenth century they were banned from public office, from the law, from the university and from keeping schools. The large numbers of new settlers were Protestant English and Scottish Dissenters, and they were never assimilated as previous newcomers had been, because of the continuing atmosphere of repression. The Dissenters stayed up north in 'drumlin' country, the small and poor hills of Monaghan, Cavan, Leitrim and Donegal.

Oliver Cromwell butchered his way through Ireland to crush a Catholic rebellion that centred upon the city of Kilkenny. There you can still climb the ancient round tower beside the cathedral, sit in the seat where he viewed five counties and look at the font he is supposed to have used as a trough for his horses (there are several more of these about). By now, the good land belonged almost exclusively to Protestants. In 1690 William of Orange set the seal on this. Today the gable-ends in the north of Ireland show King Billy painted on his white horse at his victory on the River Boyne, and you may still see the odd white horse prancing inside a Dublin fanlight. Anti-Catholic laws and repression followed William's triumph.

By the end of the eighteenth century a lot of this repression had been relaxed by a Protestant ascendancy that had itself relaxed into a new spirit of liberalism. Irish industry and Irish artefacts showed increasing skills and beauty. Great political leaders like Henry Flood and Henry Grattan led the Irish parliament towards a state of almost complete independence from England in the last two decades of the century, but the 1790s saw the rise, under Theobald Wolfe Tone's inspiration, of the United Irishmen, a society dedicated to establishing full independence, by force if necessary. Behind Tailors' Hall in Dublin, Wolfe Tone called his secret 'Back Lane Parliament' of anti-Crown conspirators. In 1798 an ill-fated French expedition in support of the United Irishmen and an equally disastrous rebellion in Wexford finally gave the parliament at Westminster an excuse for the introduction of the 1800 Act of Union which extinguished the Irish parliament.

Although 1798 had seen the ultimate end of the United Irishmen and the execution of the rebel Lord Edward Fitzgerald, there was yet another ill-fated rising in 1803. Its leader, Robert Emmet, was captured and executed in Thomas Street, outside St Catherine's Church, but while on the run he had hidden in Dublin's oldest pub, the Brazen Head, which still stands in Bridge Street near the River Liffey. As almost always, the rebels were Protestants and members of the landed gentry: a recurring pattern in the past history of Irish rebels.

In 1829 Daniel O'Connell achieved emancipation for Catholics when he secured for them the right to become members of the parliament at Westminster. Alas, it was of very little use to most Catholics during the black and dreadful decades that followed: the potato blight killed off the only crop that many country people had, leaving close on a million people to die of sheer starvation in 1846–48 and another million to emigrate – mostly to North America.

O
tell me all about
Anna Livia!
I want to hear all
about Anna Livia.

Well, you know Anna Livia?
Yes, of course we all know Anna Livia.
Tell me all.
Tell me now.

James Joyce, *Finnegan's Wake*

Anna Livia is Joyce's name for the Liffey.

Republican movements continued nevertheless to carry on the ideals of the United Irishmen. For instance, Oscar Wilde's mother, 'Speranza' Elgee, used to write for the newspapers of the Young Irelanders, while a more militant form of Fenianism, or militant Catholic nationalism, gave birth to the Irish Republican Brotherhood. In 1879 a one-armed unlettered peasant by the name of Michael Davitt founded a mass movement called the Land League, with the aim of winning back the land for those who worked on it, away from the absentee landlord who was so much the rule all over the island.

Isaac Butt was the man who inaugurated the home-rule movement in 1870. Chief among its parliamentary supporters was Charles Stewart Parnell, who became an MP in 1875 and managed to unite the nationalist movements, including the Land League, behind him. His activities helped to persuade Gladstone to introduce the Home Rule Bill in 1886, but it was fiercely resisted by the Protestants of the north-east, who had grown prosperous during the industrial revolution and who alone on the island had suffered little from famine and emigration. Parnell himself was disgraced in 1890 by the scandalous revelation of his affair with an army officer's wife, Kitty O'Shea, and died in 1891 before any real progress had been made. By the time the third Bill went to the Commons the Ulster Protestants had organised an armed resistance force under Sir Edward Carson, but in spite of their efforts the Act came into force in 1914, only to be suspended by the Great War. Many thousands of Irishmen from both North and South enlisted – including those who supported Home Rule, acting on the advice of their leader John Redmond. Whole streets of men, including those from the poorest parts of Belfast and Dublin, marched off to die on the Somme and at Passchendaele; the slaughter was incalculable (and may be part of the explanation for Southern neutrality during the last war).

And here recurred the old theme, that history is akin to poetry in complexion. As Professor Emyr Estyn Evans put it, 'There is a deep conviction in this far western isle that man has fallen from grace, that the Golden Age lies in the past; and that national glory can be restored to an imaginary state of purity, but only if men act like the heroes of their legends.'

At Easter in 1916 Patrick Pearse and James Connolly organised an armed uprising. With only around 1,000 men, they knew they were virtually certain of defeat, and yet they took Dublin's General Post Office in O'Connell Street and several key positions and held them against the British Army for about a week. You can still see the bullet holes in the pillars outside the Post Office.

The uprising did not enjoy much broad popular support until its leaders were executed by the British armed forces – James Connolly in a chair, due to the fact that he had been wounded in the leg. The results of the next general election in 1918 showed a massive swing away from Redmond's Irish Parliamentary Party towards the Independence Party of Sinn Fein ('We Ourselves'), which won 73 out of 105 seats. In short, the Army fuelled public opinion heavily against the government by shooting the seven rebel signers of the provisional proclamation of independence at the GPO, as well as another nine men who had not signed.

The Sinn Fein leader Eamon de Valera had escaped execution because of his American birth. Under his presidency a provisional government was called into being, and a military wing under Michael Collins and Cathal Brugha set out to wage a war of independence.

In 1920 the Government of Ireland Act was passed at Westminster, giving a separate parliament for the counties of Antrim, Armagh, Derry, Down, Fermanagh and Tyrone. This was the parliament at Stormont outside Belfast, which collapsed during the troubles of the seventies: now the six counties are ruled from London once again.

In 1921 Michael Collins and Arthur Griffith went to London to negotiate the Treaty with England. The articles of agreement which they signed established the Irish Free State as a dominion of the British Commonwealth, but allowed the six northern counties the choice of opting for Britain – an option they instantly plumped for.

In the South meanwhile civil war broke out between those who disagreed with the terms of the Treaty and felt that a claim should have been kept on all thirty-two counties and those who supported the Treaty-signers. During this civil war both Michael Collins and Cathal Brugha were killed in ambushes. The 'Soldiers of Destiny' or Fianna Fáil party, which opposed partition, was born under de Valera out of the Sinn Fein movement. The Fine Gael ('We Gaels') party was pro-Treaty. (The terms Fianna Fáil and Fine Gael given to today's two major parties bear no relation to a left-right political spectrum, by the way, but relate back to this bitter time.)

Today's Irish parliament is known as the Dáil, and it returns 148 members to its assembly at Leinster House in Kildare Street, Dublin, as well as 60 senators to the Senate or higher house. The assembly is called the Oireachtas and has an elected president, as well as a taoiseach, or prime minister, who is the head of the majority party. The constitution adopted by the Dáil is the constitution that Eamon de Valera presented in 1937 and which was adopted by referendum. It has two very controversial passages; in one article it lays claim to the six counties of the North, and in another it gives a special place to the Roman Catholic religion. While there is a strong body of opinion in the Irish Republic which feels that these articles should be deleted, it would almost certainly cause more trouble than it would ever eliminate.

In the last few years the social services and training schemes for the young have improved beyond all recognition in the South of Ireland, while still being far lower than the generally accepted EEC norms. It is no longer compulsory to learn Irish, which means that it is now a little more popular with young people. The fact that there are now five television channels on the east coast and two on the west, as well as two government radio stations, means that as a country Ireland is progressively less and less isolated.

But it will be another while before Ireland lines up and resembles the other member countries of the Common Market. Cynics would say that it will take many more years for her phones to work as they do in other countries, for her roads to be improved, and for the public transport to operate as it does elsewhere in the world. There is a recognisable claustrophobia about living in a country so small, as well as a beguiling intimacy. As the old saying has it: '*Is i scath a cheile a mhaireann na ndaoine*', 'People live in each other's shadows', and sometimes it is this that holds the country back – the great hatred and little room, as Yeats put it.

'The Irish are a very fair race – they never speak well of each other', said George Bernard Shaw, one of Ireland's fiercest critics, and born in Synge Street, Dublin. It is true that for really trenchant criticism of Irish institutions and the Irish way of life you have only to go to an Irishman. But at the same time, criticism from a foreigner brings out the opposite emotion:

> *Nil aon tin tean*
> *Mar do thintean fein.*

'There's no fireplace like your own fireplace.'

Elgy Gillespie

It was to these shores of Antrim, near the White Arch, that the firstcomers made their way, hunters and fishermen attracted by the flints and by the thickly forested island just a few miles away. Later on the legends – the Children of Lir, Deirdre and the sons of Uisneach – emerged from this corner of the island.

On the northern coast of the island is the weird and solitary Giant's Causeway (*left*): not man-made, as people used to think three centuries ago, but a natural phenomenon that can be seen in other places in the world. Never quite so massively as here, though, where the white-hot lava flow that once covered the cold surface beneath it shrank and split into the serried ranks of three- to nine-sided columns. Some sheer up together like organ-pipes: others like a fan. Dr Johnson's verdict was 'Worth seeing – but not worth going to see' when he and Boswell made the then painful journey.

On the road from Portrush to Portballintrae is the dramatically placed fourteenth-century castle of Dunluce. Part of it fell into the sea, carrying servants with it, in the seventeenth century. Immediately afterwards it was attacked by the reassembled Gaels, and a year after that, its incumbent, the Earl of Antrim, was arrested by one of his guests, General Monroe.

Lammas Fair (*below*) is the August feastday for Antrim sheepfarmers when 'Yellowman', a type of chewy toffee made to an old recipe, is still eaten among all the hustlers and stalls of Ballycastle, a bustling coastal resort with long sandy beaches.

The many blends of Irish whiskey are kept distinct, though all are now sheltered by the umbrella of Irish Distillers, whose brand-new headquarters are in Midleton, County Cork. But up in the tiny village of Bushmills (*bottom*) near Coleraine the oldest and – according to many connoisseurs – the finest blend of all is still distilled in buildings that go back to the seventeenth century. Try Black Label 'Bush' for a veritable liqueur of a whiskey.

The small Antrim fishing village of Ballintoy.

To reach Rathlin Island you have to hire a motor-boat from Ballycastle, Antrim, to take you the five miles across. It was the first spot in Ireland to be attacked by the Vikings, and it was here that Robert the Bruce first found refuge from the English, after his ignominious defeat as King of Scotland. The Irish spoken around here is the Gaelic that Scottish Highlanders would understand, and it was here that the story of Bruce and his spider took place.

Before the last century Belfast was occasionally described as 'a village not far from Carrickfergus', and the latter's fame in song goes back centuries as the most convenient landing-point from Scotland. 'I wish I was in Carrickfergus . . .' goes an exile's lament, and this town with its dramatically sited twelfth-century castle ingrained itself on emigrants and immigrants alike. King Billy landed here before his march to the Boyne. At present the fine Norman castle houses a military museum.

Charles Lanyon was the man responsible for the most interesting Victorian buildings in Victorian Belfast and its Malone Road campus purlieus. Queen's University (*below*) is no exception: its charming redbrick mock-Tudor nonsensicalities extend to the Gothic library by S. F. Lynn, his disciple and pupil, which has a cathedral-height vaulted ceiling and gargoyles in its guttering. The central tower he intended as an echo of the Founder's Tower of Magdalen College, Oxford.

Belfast is in every way a flower of late Victorianism. While Dublin bloomed in the eighteenth century and then decayed once more, Belfast had to wait for the Industrial Revolution and the heyday of the linen trade, until finally the expansion of the Empire meant that of her dockyards. It was a triumphal era of history, and her buildings reflect this mood. The centrepiece is the City Hall (*right above and below*) at the end of Royal Avenue. It is the work of Alfred Brumwell Thomas who finished it in 1906 and whose over-elaborated style is sometimes mocked by Belfastmen. Its central Ionic dome is 173ft high and flanked by twin smaller domes. The statue of Queen Victoria was unveiled by King Edward in 1903, and he is supposed to have commented: 'Couldn't be better!' During one rag week, his mother had giant phantom footsteps painted by an invisible nocturnal vandal down the side of her pedestal, across the pavement and down the steps of the ladies' toilet!

The Northern Ireland Parliament Building at Stormont (*below*) presents to the visitor a plain classical facade. Built in the years between 1928 and 1932, it contrasts nicely with the Scottish baronial style of nearby Stormont Castle, which houses various government departments.

The shapes of the shipyard (*right*) could be said to shape the memories of all Belfastmen; they symbolise the days when Belfast was world-famous for its shipbuilding and a whole city's pride was built, and sank, with the *Titanic*. As orders grow fewer and capital investment diminishes and more men are laid off, the yards acquire a more and more poignant air. They have always been a focus of political debate, and are still. You could say the shipyards are Belfast.

Used as a location for Carol Reed's film *Odd Man
Out*, in which a wounded IRA man on the run
played by Robert Newton hides in one of its snugs,
the Crown Liquor Saloon is undeniably the most
quixotic public house in these islands. Its pillars are
carved into gilded palm trees, its snugs guarded by
carved lions and griffins bearing shields that say
'*Verus Amor Patriae*' and '*Audaces Fortuna Juvat*'
and the windows are of richly stained glass. The
bombings damaged the fittings and made for early
closing: but now the National Trust have bought
the pub and are fully restoring it.

Minnowburn Bridge, near Belfast.

The name Annalong (*see pages 36–37*) means the
ford of the ships, perhaps the longships of the
Vikings. It was an attraction for invaders because of
its natural harbour of indented rock, now
surrounded by fishermen's stone harbour walls
draped with nets, themselves in turn surrounded by
small cottages from which a watchful eye may be
kept upon the masts of small half-decks and
trawlers. There is even a rubble-built mill
with wheel.

Annalong (*see caption on page 35*).

Because Lord and Lady Bangor could not agree
about the style of Castleward back in the eighteenth
century they built the south side in Classical style
and the north side in Gothick (*below left*), with
three storeys and seven bays of ogee windows. While
its salons and kitchens are open to the public, its
stables are popular for concerts and recitals as well,
and it is one of the prouder possessions of the
National Trust of Northern Ireland.

Hillsborough is so pretty a town and so carefully
maintained and restored that it is rapidly becoming
a favourite home for fashionable commuters. In
1758 the tireless correspondent Mrs Delany
mentions Lord Hillsborough's problems with the
ancestral home (*above right*) of his family, laid out
by Colonel Arthur Hill in 1650: 'the old castle is
fallen to decay but as it is a testimony of the
antiquity of his family he is determined to keep it
up.' It is now the property of the state.

Armagh's two cathedrals confront each other
defiantly and almost embarrassingly upon the two
main hills within the ancient earthfort upon which
the old ecclesiastical capital of Ireland was set. By
all accounts it was Patrick himself who built the first
church here in the sixth century, but the present
simple, almost austere Protestant cathedral is a
nineteenth-century renovation. On the other hill is
J. J. McCarthy's Catholic cathedral (*below*), begun
in 1840, with its Italian 'angel' ceiling, topping a
stairway that hints at the biblical Jacob's ladder.

Gortin Glen, County Tyrone.

40

It was Lord Mount Florence, ancestor of the earls of Enniskillen, who built Florence Court (*below*) in 1764 – but much about it remains mysterious. Was the architect the Sardinian whose name, curiously enough, was Davis Ducart and who was so fashionable at the time? Was the plasterwork by the Dublin stuccoer Robert West? A bad fire in 1955 left it seriously wrecked, but it has been restored by the National Trust. Just four miles away are the vast and melodramatic caves of limestone known as the Marble Arch caves, which cross the border below ground and have not yet been fully explored.

Evidence of the school of stone masonry that sprang up upon the shores of Lough Erne abounds in the carved heads of the Devenish Island and White Island churches. In White Island (*right above*) the mask of a human and eight more weird figures have been built into the wall of the Romanesque church; one is an abbot but the others seem to be soldiers or

warriors clad in the early Irish manner. Similar heads are built into the wall of the Devenish round tower (*right below*) and in the museum there the early stonemasons, whose tradition appears to have waxed and waned with the supply of stone and the continuity of a religious community over the centuries, are documented. In Enniskillen there is further material on them in the county museum.

The name 'Derry' comes from *doire*, the word for an oak grove in Irish, and Derry (or Londonderry) is said to be where St Columba had his own grove. Invariably known as 'Derry' to all who live there, of either persuasion, the city (*right and below*) was sorely scarred in the bombing, though its casualty list was never quite as bitter and grievous as that of Belfast or some small towns like Claudy. It is, as cities go, exceptionally merry and lovable and marked deeply by love of song as well as by unemployment of a higher percentage than almost anywhere else in Europe. Emigration for the menfolk has always been the only solution. Recent excitements include the whale that battered its way up the Foyle and frolicked beneath the bridge that connects the Waterside to the city and Bogside.

Near the resort of Castlerock is the little folly tossed in as a postscript by the eccentric Lord Bristol, Bishop of Derry. Mussenden Temple (*left*) was probably designed by the Cork-born architect Michael Shanahan and was named after the bishop's cousin. His famous collection and house have long since perished, but the little temple still sits upon its characteristically romantic cliff-top site.

Malin Head, the northernmost point of Ireland.

Mount Errigal (*below*) rises from the heart of the
Donegal Gaeltacht, where an Irish very like the
Scottish Gaelic is spoken. It is the highest mountain
in Donegal, which still makes it a mere 2466ft, and
its quartzite glinting facets are scattered with scree
that gives the mountaineer a tedious climb but a
splendid view. The nearest town is Gweedore.

Killybegs (*right*) is a bustling little port that has
repaid all the investments that have gone into its
fishing fleets many times over. Big inshore trawlers
of over 70ft are built here to garner the herring
catch, though this has not been a big one in recent
years. But fishermen now earn very well for their
hard times at sea. It is a happy little town with a
good pub life and good fresh fish for tea.

Sheep Haven, Donegal.

Tory (*above*) is an island with an added dimension of isolation because of its distance from the shore – 11 miles – and the frequent bad weather that cuts its 265-strong population off for weeks at a time. It has difficulty in getting a teacher for its school and is petitioning for an airstrip to take regular flights. There is no doctor, and women fly to the mainland several weeks before babies are due. The 'cursing stones', say islanders, are what helped them resist the rates collectors in the last century: they are an archaeological curiosity to match Balar's Fort, named after a local giant in myth. There is a flourishing school of naive painting here headed by the Dixons (father and son) and Rogers (uncle and nephew).

Gortahork (*right*) lies in the Donegal Gaeltacht at the head of Ballyness Bay.

Ballyness Bay, Donegal.

Glencolumbkille is a village blessed with proud and active people whose aim it is to make it a home for craftworkers and a home-from-home for visitors. You can rent a cottage here from the local co-operative as well as buy jewellery, pottery, knits or weaving. It is also the site of megalithic and Early Christian remains, which include a huge cairn and a chamber tomb, as well as several later ringforts with clochans or cells within them and many carved pillarstones (*below*) of the Early Christian era.

An Irish fiddler is always ready to entertain.

The Dartry Mountains (*right*) rise abruptly just to
the north of Sligo. The highest peak is Truskmore
(2113ft), while to the west is Benbulbin, a familiar
sight across Sligo Bay. W. B. Yeats certainly knew
it, for this is Yeats country and he wrote of it in
Under Ben Bulben (*see page 60*).

Under bare Ben Bulben's head
In Drumcliff churchyard Yeats is laid.
An ancestor was rector there
Long years ago, a church stands near,
By the road an ancient cross.
No marble, no conventional phrase;
On limestone quarried near the spot
By his command these words are cut:

> *Cast a cold eye*
> *On life, on death.*
> *Horseman, pass by!*

W. B. Yeats

Yeats died in Roquebrune in 1939, but his remains
were not brought back to Drumcliff churchyard for
another ten years. The epitaph on his tombstone
there consists of the last three lines of his poem
Under Ben Bulben, quoted here.

Benbulbin (*right*).

'Leitrim – where the sparrows drop off the twigs from hunger' is an epithet that used to describe the tiny scratching farms and closed perspectives of what was always thought to be the poorest county – if at times also the most beautiful, as here (*below*) in Glencar. But vigorous local entrepreneurism means that the farmers on mean soil are no longer so very small: those that have survived and have not emigrated are now comfortable Europeanised agri-businessmen outside.

Lough Key, Roscommon (*right*).

The Midlands lakes are often named after ancient gods and goddesses or animals from the myths, and crannogs and ringfort remains in abundance show that this must have been a populous spot in pre-Christian days. On Lough Oughter (*below right*) you will find the romantic castle of the medieval Gaelic O'Reillys, where died the much-mourned Owen Roe O'Neill.

Granard is an unassuming little market town, at the
strategic centre of the Midlands lakes between
Longford and Cavan. 'The highest tillage land in all
Ireland' is how the locals describe the environs of
the town and their rich alluvial soil. That still does
not make it remarkably high, though it does have
two interesting stone circles nearby and a good
Norman mote and bailey, courtesy of Hugh
de Lacy.

The Shannon runs for 234 miles from North to South and covers the counties of Leitrim, Roscommon, Galway (all in Connaught), Longford (*below*), Offaly and Meath (Leinster) and finally Tipperary, Clare, Limerick and Kerry (Munster) before it slowly pours into the Atlantic. Almost all the way it can be navigated by large vessels, a majestic river of great depth and gentle current. Its possibilities as a pleasure pathway for cabin-cruising holidaymakers are just beginning to be realised.

Trim Castle (*below*) dominates the Norman town of Trim upon the banks of the Boyne and has a stormy history dating back to Hugh de Lacy, first of the horse-riding mercenaries with their tightly formed ranks to conquer Meath. King John came here and, nearly two centuries later, Richard II stayed and left Prince Hal (Henry V) and Humphrey of Gloucester. The town walls used to touch the castle walls, but by 1599 it was in ruins, though Cromwell's army took the trouble to storm it during their stay, an indication of their thoroughness.

The market cross in Kells town (*below*) shows scenes from the Bible and, according to local belief, was used as a gallows in the 1798 rising.

Newgrange retains its mystery as an ancient centre of ritual and burial rites, commanding a view of the lush valley of the Boyne from its height. It is one of the very finest examples of a prehistoric passage-grave (*bottom*) in Europe and is the best-known of all Ireland's megalithic monuments. The body of the mound is circled with upright stones up to 10ft in height, tooled with zigzags, spirals and lozenges. Inside, the chamber is cruciform and again the uprights are carved. It dates to 2500 BC but was used long afterwards by the 'Beaker' folk, who may also have found the fact that sunlight strikes the final upright on the shortest day of the year useful when consulting their calendar. New facts are emerging about it as archaeologists make fresh finds.

Monasterboice (*below*) is most known as a watering hole for the weary traveller on his way to Dublin or to Belfast: but it was originally the spot where a sixth-century monastery was founded, afterwards victim of a Viking attack and a counterattack by Domnall, King of Tara. Its cross, erected in the tenth century, is known as the Cross of Muiredach and is one of the very finest in the country, with Adam and Eve, Cain and Abel, David and Goliath, Moses smiting the rock, the Adoration of the Magi, Christ in glory with Michael to weigh the good and

bad souls surrounding him and all the episodes of the Crucifixion – every one being a scene traditional to High Cross carving.

Croagh Patrick, the holy mountain in Mayo (*right*).

Lough Mask (*below right*) has the ruins of a seventh-century monastery and also some prehistoric earthworks. Captain Charles Boycott, who lived near here, gave his name to the dictionary when people around there cold-shouldered him.

Turf-cutting is a summer job that until recently
even some Dublin families used to do, renting turf-
cuts in the nearby hills to supply themselves for the
winter. It requires a special sideways-facing cutting
spade called a slane and a methodical method of
spreading, turning, footing, stacking and drying the
sods the old way, to make sure they will light easily.
The great boglands of the west are still fuel-
providers for many a country home.

Gaelic football, like its more graceful brother game
of hurling, is an old Irish sport dating back to
earliest times. It outdoes any soccer match for
roughness, brio and attack and is much nearer
American football. The league is organised by the
Gaelic Athletic Association or GAA who forbade
players any non-Irish games until recently – the
others being handball, a sort of pelota played
against a high enclosed wall, and camogie, a girls'
game like a rougher form of hockey.

The Twelve Bens.

Four miles from Loughrea stands the famous Turoe Stone (*left*), the best relic of the La Tène phase of Celtic art of around the first century, and one of only four similar stones. Phallic in shape, it is tooled with Celtic curvilinear patterns.

The salmon that used to swim upstream into Lough Corrib (*below*) in their thousands, beating their way up the rapids in an attempt to gain their spawning grounds over in the lakes and streams, are now a rarer sight. At one time you could see them almost packed shoulder to shoulder, nose to stream, waiting just below the bridge in Galway for the rain so that the water-level would rise high enough to let them pass. Small wonder that the salmon is so prominent in ancient Irish mythology, and a symbol of wisdom like the one in the Finn Mac Cool legends.

Clonfert Cathedral (*right*), and in particular its enormous portal, is the finest flowering of the Irish Romanesque style in church architecture, dating back mainly to the twelfth and thirteenth centuries since the previous seventh-century foundation built by the son of Brendan the Navigator had been several times over destroyed by Vikings or by fires.

Clifden, a favourite touring centre for exploring Connemara and the Twelve Bens.

Traditional transport here is the currach (*left*).

Dún Aengus (*below left*), a superb pre-Christian promontory fort.

The Aran Islanders (*below*) vary markedly from the mainlanders: curiously, many of them belong to blood group A while O is the mainland norm and they are temperamentally quite different, noted for their adventurousness. Legend has it that they are descended from some of Cromwell's soldiers and survived the Famine on fish. Their powers of survival have always been tested to the very limit on the stone-strewn, almost soil-less limestone outcrops that make up the isles. They carefully fertilised the tiny wall-riddled fields with sand and seaweed till they had enough for potatoes, oats and a bit of grass for the cattle, but their individual and highly original way of life was until recently threatened by lack of communications and emigration and the usual joblessness. Now their population is on the up and up again, together with their fishing and their tourism trade.

The Cliffs of Moher tower 668ft above the Atlantic at their highest point, presenting the natural fortress that the Spaniards must have seen looming as they searched for a safe berth. They eventually found one in nearby Liscannor. O'Brien's Tower on the clifftop gives a panorama of the Aran Islands and Connemara.

The Ennistymon Falls are the pride of the Spa Hotel and the small County Clare town of Ennistymon, not far from Lahinch, where their water-powered pumps provide the hotel with power for heating through the winter.

The Burren is famous among botanists as a freak geological phenomenon which has given rise to types of alpine flora (*left*). It is made up of great flattened beds of scored limestone, porous and deeply fissured and minus a single tree or clump of soil in the higher parts. Its streams, the Caher and the Fergus, hold a rare pondweed, but it is the alpine gentian and the dense-flowered orchid, the maidenhair and the moss saxifrages that keep the botanists coming back here–though insecticides have made their inroads here as everywhere else.

Poulnabrone Dolmen (*above*) is one of the better examples of the portal dolmens in which megalithic man buried his dead. The three or more standing stones were covered with a large capstone. There are several other prehistoric burial sites here, near Ballyvaughan in County Clare.

The horse-drawn plough (*left*) is now a rare sight. Common Market subventions have meant a great influx of modern farm machinery.

Bunratty Castle (*left*), well known for its medieval banquets where tourists flock to eat soup in bowls without handles and drink lethal goblets of mead.

Killaloe, on the Shannon (*below left*).

Limerick (*below*) is a city that is much abused by the Irish themselves for its air of seedy dereliction. In fact it is capable of being both mysterious and romantic. Its tragedy is that, though it was built proudly and magnificently upon a grandiose scale in the eighteenth century, and was to become one of Western Europe's major sea-ports, it fell a victim to the political and social tragedies of the nineteenth century. They ate into Limerick's talents and prospects; the economic decline that followed ensured that in spite of her size Limerick remained a country town in her mentality. If you wander down to the section of Parish on the banks of the Shannon you will find a quite different Limerick, reminiscent of her Viking and Norman past.

A violinmaker, the essential craftsman behind the
ubiquitous Irish fiddler.

Cahir Castle sits upon a rock-isle in the River Suir,
a large-scale fifteenth-century castle built by the
powerful Butler family. It played a very active part
in Elizabeth I's Plantation when she sent her Lord
Lieutenant, the Earl of Essex, to besiege it.

Slea Head on the Dingle peninsula.

Dingle is a fishing centre in the Kerry Gaeltacht or
Irish-speaking region. Director David Lean made
Ryan's Daughter here, complete with a reconstructed
village that has since been sold abroad!

Traditional toil in a potato field.

Dunquin altar boys. After a long struggle the tiny two-room Irish-speaking school was re-opened here a few years ago, so boys and girls no longer have to go away to school.

Irish pigs have to be fit!

Gallarus Oratory is a little Early Christian church
of unknown date near the Irish-speaking town of
Ballyferriter on the Dingle peninsula, with dry-
stone walls and a corbelled roof. Its neat
symmetrical shape follows the most ancient
building methods.

Killarney Lakes (*see caption on page 96*).

The Killarney Lakes (*below and pages 94–5*) were
much admired by Queen Victoria. Lough Leane,
Muckross Lake and Upper Lake lie at the foot of
MacGillycuddy's Reeks and offer a circuit of the
celebrated 'Ring' via Aghadoe and Beaufort Bridge
to Kate Kearney's cottage in the Gap of Dunloe and
then through the Gap and on by boat back to Lough
Leane. The native strawberry tree or *Arbutus unedo*
grows well here because of the mildness of the rainy
warmth wafted over Kerry by the Gulf Stream;
there are also rare ferns.

Biddyboys (*left*) are a Kerry phenomenon and, like the Swords mummers near Dublin and the strawberry men of County Wexford, they have their own dances dating back to the Middle Ages.

Puck Fair or the Aonach an Phuic (*below*) takes place every August in the small Kerry town of Killorglin, when the puck or specially chosen white and beribboned billy-goat is perched boisterously above a milling massing crowd of revellers upon the top of a special column for the space of a weekend.

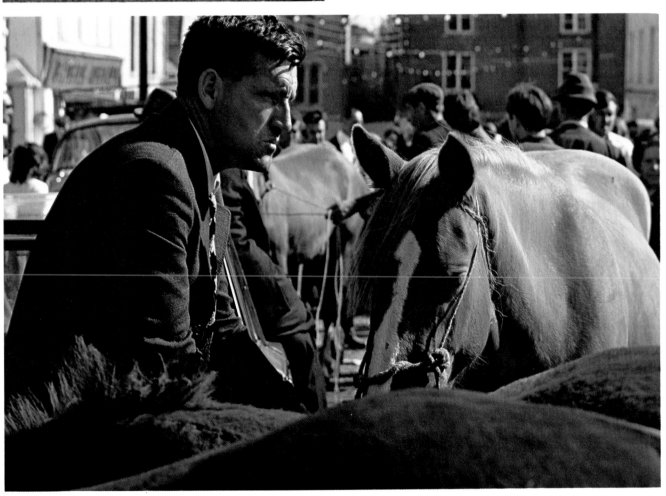

MacGillycuddy's Reeks (*left*) are the highest mountain range in Ireland, separated from Killarney town by the Gap of Dunloe. Tightly-packed peaks flanked by water and other mountains, they may be reached from Caragh Lake and Glencar.

Near Caherdaniel with Deenish and Scariff Islands (*below*).

Garinish Island (*see pages 100–1*) is where George Bernard Shaw came to write *Saint Joan*: an exotic garden laid out in the Classical Italian style by a landscapist called Peto early this century. He was helped by the mildening effect of the Gulf Stream.

Garinish Island
(*see caption on page 99*).

Kissing the stone in Blarney Castle is a relatively
recent idea, coming from nobody knows where. It
was also quite difficult till a few years ago, since it
meant leaning backwards high above the tree-level
to apply your lips to a very wet-looking patch on an
outer wall. Now it has been made simpler, and in
theory this will mean that the visitor will never be
stuck for words again . . .

A stone that whoever kisses
O, he never misses to grow eloquent . . .

The Sheep's Head pokes its way out into the Atlantic, to face the New World far across the waters.

The bells of Shandon
That sound so grand on
The pleasant waters
Of the River Lee . . .

So runs Father Prout's
ditty about St Anne's
Protestant parish church
in the Cork district of
Shandon (*right*). Its
tower houses the famous
bells of Shandon which
any visitor can play.

The third largest city in the island and the second largest city of the Republic, Cork is always thought of as the first capital by her own citizens! Supposedly founded by the early Christian saint Finnbarr, she straddles the channels of the River Lee (*below left*) around a series of small islands, and many of her major streets were watercourses until recent centuries, including Patrick Street or *Panna* as it is known. This has contributed to making it an agreeably Italianate, architecturally southern sort of city of great pleasantness.

St Finnbarr's cathedral (*below*) commemorates the legendary founder of Cork City, an extravagant French-Gothic building of the last century by William Burges. It replaces a Georgian cathedral that in turn replaced a medieval one which probably in turn supplanted several others.

The River Blackwater (*below*) flows out to sea at Youghal, a pretty little medieval town with fine walls. Raleigh had a house here, Myrtle Grove, and Shakespeare's acting company used to come over on visits: whether he came with them is not known.

Pub cum undertaker (*right above*).

Hurling (*bottom*) is a fast-moving game played with curved sticks made from ash known as *camans*. The game is first mentioned in 'The Cattle Raid of Cooley' (*Tain bo Cuailgne*), the body of legends from the Ulster Cycle in which the feats of Cuchulain are related. A young boy called Setanta kills the Ulster king's watchdog by whacking a hurley-ball down his throat, after successfully taking on over a hundred young hurley-wielding youths. After this feat he becomes Cuchulain, the hound of Ulster. Kilkenny and Cork are the two most famous hurling counties.

Tinkers (*far left*) are also known as travellers, the word they use to describe themselves now that they are doing no more 'tinking' or pot- and pan-mending from door to door as in the old days. Gradually they have lost all forms of livelihood other than begging, trading and horse-dealing, and though they still tour the country in caravans, more and more gather to beg in the city centres. More are settling in one place than before, but they are often moved on by hostile townfolk who resent their wandering horses, their ragged children, the second-hand clothes sprayed over their surroundings and the unchanging cry of 'Wouldja ever have a penny for the little baby, mister?' All this has prevented people from finding out very much about them or their language and customs; they have almost no oral history, but they do have their own vocabulary and their own songs.

The Fall of Adam and Eve (*left*) in St Declan's, Ardmore, one of the Romanesque west gable carvings of Bible scenes; it belongs to the thirteenth century.

A country fair at Tallow, Waterford (*below*).

Jerpoint Abbey lies just outside the lovely little
town of Thomastown on the River Nore in
Kilkenny, a Cistercian monastery with unusually
interesting carvings.

The Dunmore Caves have a place in mythology as the home of Luchtigern, King of the Mice. More sinisterly, many skeletons have been found there, mostly of women and children. Very likely they huddled in the caves for safety and were discovered and killed by Vikings, for several very interesting Viking coins—including a dirham brought back from an Eastern caliphate by some Viking trader—were found upon the cave floor. The cave, now open to the public, can be reached from the Castlecomer Road.

Kilkenny Castle overlooks the River Nore and the city of Kilkenny that sits both sides of its banks. It was said to have been started by the Norman mercenary Strongbow, and then completed by William the Marshall. It can at any rate lay claim to 700 years of continuous occupation. At the moment it has art galleries and a recital room, while the stables house the Kilkenny Design Workshops and shops.

Though there are few blacksmiths (*right*) left in the country areas, there are some and there are even more empty forges.

In the Great Picture Gallery of Kilkenny Castle, designed by Benjamin Woodward, a brilliant friend of Ruskin from Cork, are these hammer beams (*right below*) with evocations of the Bible. They echo the medieval beams of the cathedral at the other end of the town.

Tynans (*below*) was once a grocery like so many country town pubs. It still owns its original gaslights, and Michael and Freda Tynan have kept the little mahogany drawers from which seeds and crystallised fruits were once sold.

St Canice's (*left*), overlooking the section of Kilkenny known as Irishtown, sits on its mound surrounded by the Deanery, the Bishop's Palace and the library. The round tower is the sole survivor of its Early Christian days. The rest of the cathedral dates to the thirteenth century and was simple and dignified in the medieval style; in spite of history's many vicissitudes it remains pretty much the same, with its fluted Norman font that Cromwell is supposed to have used as a horse-trough and its many monuments to the Ormonde Butler family. Now it is often used for concerts, and its acoustics have been carefully adjusted to accommodate Schubert *Lieder* and Mahler symphonies.

Stradbally Steam Museum contains early motorcars,
locomotives, fire engines and all early train
machinery; they hold an open day every August.

The River Barrow is navigable down to New Ross and can be travelled by 'narrow' boat, through the little locks of County Kildare and on past peaceful little villages like St Mullins in County Carlow.

Glendalough (*left*) is a beauty spot that is easily reached from Dublin: an Early Christian monastery set at the top of two lakes in a narrow valley, with a round tower and a cathedral and a 'priest's house'. It was begun by St Kevin, a seventh-century hermit who so wished to renounce the world that he asked people not to settle near his cell. There is also a story that he requested a virgin from the nearest community to stand before him naked while he wrestled with temptation, then thrust her into the lake and ensured his immortal soul.

The hunt (*below left*) is still popular all over Ireland.

Though Powerscourt House (*below*) was very badly burnt some years ago, it still makes another of the favourite day drips from Dublin with its waterfall and Japanese garden plus deerpark and wooded demesne, all backed by the Wicklow mountains. The eighteenth-century woods are of beech and chestnut and oak.

White's Castle in the town of Athy was built in 1575, and its name commemorates James, the 'White' Earl of Desmond and Lieutenant of the King of England who wiped out many of the O'More family near here in battle.

Clonmacnoise (*left*) is an Early Christian monastic community started by St Ciaran in the sixth century, and now carefully restored. Masses are still said here in the open air. Its enclosure holds seven churches, three good High Crosses, two round towers and many carved early grave-slabs.

Fishing for salmon on the Liffey (*below*).

The Four Courts were begun by James Gandon in
1787, and the building fronts the river for 450ft
with its six massive columns and huge dome. It was
the site of a battle during the Civil War, in which
the public records were almost all burnt. With this
building downstream and the lighter, more marine
Custom House upstream, Gandon set his seal
surely upon the Dublin skyline.

The Custom House was very nearly built in
Leningrad because Leningrad is where its architect,
James Gandon, originally wanted to go until that
particular job fell through and he took on the task of
modelling Dublin instead. It took many troubled
years to finish; begun in 1781, it boasts over the
windows fourteen specially carved heads by Edward
Smyth representing all the rivers.

In the second half of the eighteenth century Dublin hit a welcome era of expansion, and a great building period led by architects like Edward Lovett Pearce and Richard Cassels brought in the golden rule that translated the former walled medieval city into squares and terraces of pink-bricked lofty grace, north and south of the River Liffey. In the last decade the city centre has suffered grievously from planning blight and unsympathetic development, whereas before it suffered merely from poverty and decay. Nowadays the Georgian architecture of the south side (*left and below*) is on the whole very lovingly cared for–with some exceptions. But this is still not the case on the north side, unfortunately.

It was J. P. Donleavy, author of *The Ginger Man*, who once remarked that the pubs of Dublin (*right*) are like a series of rooms into which different combinations of people enter, changing at an ungiven cue till at last they all seem to converge upon the same one.

In August the Horse Show (*right*) brings the country and the hoi polloi alike into the Royal Dublin Society grounds for the jumping.

This (*bottom*) is the O'Caseyesque side of old Dublin that is almost gone, along with the old Moore Street stalls, though its spirit lives on.

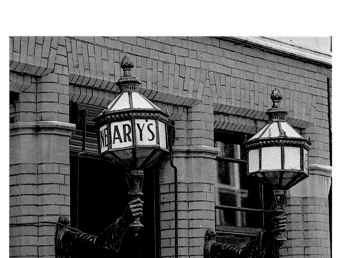

Trinity College is a mini-kingdom of itself in the
middle of the busiest bit of central Dublin, and
there is an air of unreality about its tranquil cobbles,
campanile and the Rubricks. Its architecture spans
all eras from 1700 with distinction, and here you
may find the Book of Kells, Brian Boru's harp, a
skeleton of the giant Irish elk and fine modern art.
It has also housed Burke, Berkeley, Hume,
Goldsmith, Sheridan, Congreve, Farquhar, Wilde,
Synge, Swift, Grattan, Emmet, Tone, Davis,
Mitchel, Luby, Butt (these last all patriots) and so
on. In recent years Samuel Beckett and Conor
Cruise O'Brien have been the best-known alumni.

The Ha'penny Bridge in Dublin got its name from
the toll that was once charged to cross it. The real
name is the Metal Bridge, a single-arch cast-iron
footbridge first built in 1816. The wooden planks
are changed at regular intervals.